The Wild World of Animals

Rhinos

Horn-Faced Chargers

by Lola M. Schaefer

Consultant:
Barre E. Fields
Senior Animal Trainer
Indianapolis Zoo

Bridgestone Books
an imprint of Capstone Press
Mankato, Minnesota

105

Bridgestone Books are published by Capstone Press
١ﻟ1 Good Counsel Drive, P.O. Box 669, Mankato, Minnesota 56002
http://www.capstone-press.com

Library of Congress Cataloging-in-Publication Data
Schaefer, Lola M., 1950–
    Rhinos: horn-faced chargers/by Lola M. Schaefer.
    p. cm.—(The wild world of animals)
    Includes bibliographical references and index.
    ISBN 0-7368-0967-8
    1. Rhinoceroses—Juvenile literature. [1. Rhinoceroses.] I. Title. II. Series.
QL737.U63 S29 2002
599.66'8—dc21   00-012648

Summary: An introduction to rhinos describing their physical characteristics, habitat, young,
    food, predators, and relationship to people.

Editorial Credits
Karen L. Daas and Tom Adamson, editors; Karen Risch, product planning editor; Linda Clavel,
    designer and illustrator; Heidi Schoof, photo researcher

Photo Credits
Craig Brandt, 4
Digital Stock, cover
Index Stock Imagery, 1
Joe McDonald, 8, 16
Richard Demler, 20
Robin Brandt, 6, 14
Thomas Kitchin/TOM STACK & ASSOCIATES, 12
Tom & Pat Leeson, 10
Visuals Unlimited/Ken Lucas, 18

Table of Contents

white rhino

tail

horn

foot

nose

FUN FACTS

Rhino is short for rhinoceros. Rhino
means nose. Ceros means horn.

Rhinos

All rhinos have thick gray skin. At least one horn is on their nose. Rhinos are 4 to 6 feet (1.2 to 1.8 meters) tall at the shoulder. An adult rhino can weigh as much as 5,000 pounds (2,268 kilograms). Rhinos have three toes covered by a hoof on each foot.

FUN FACTS Rhinos cannot sweat to cool off. Instead, they swim, rest, or play in water. They sometimes roll in cool, wet mud.

white rhinos

Rhinos Are Mammals

Rhinos are mammals. Mammals are warm-blooded animals with a backbone. Adult female rhinos give birth to live young. They feed milk to their young.

warm-blooded
having a body temperature that stays the same

Indian rhino

A Rhino's Habitat

Rhinos live in different habitats. White rhinos and black rhinos roam the African plains. Indian rhinos live in swampy areas in Asia. Sumatran and Javan rhinos live in Asian forests.

habitat
the place where
an animal lives

black rhino

FUN FACTS

Black rhinos have a pointed lip. Their lip helps them grab leaves and branches.

What Do Rhinos Eat?

Rhinos are herbivores. They only eat plants. Some rhinos eat grass. Other rhinos eat tree leaves. Rhinos eat 30 to 60 pounds (14 to 27 kilograms) of plants each day. They spend about half their time eating.

Male rhinos may fight other male rhinos. They use their horns as weapons. They put their heads down and charge at each other.

black rhinos

A Rhino's Horn

All rhinos have at least one horn on their nose. The horn is made of keratin. Human hair and fingernails also have keratin. A rhino's horn may break off while it is fighting. A new horn grows to replace the broken one.

white rhinos

Mating and Birth

Rhinos make noises to attract a mate. The cow whistles. A cow is a female rhino. The bull snorts, squeals, or roars. A bull is a male rhino. A young rhino does not have a horn at birth. Its horn begins to grow after about 15 weeks.

white rhinos

FUN FACTS

White rhinos are sometimes called square-lipped rhinos. The shape of their lips helps them eat grass.

Calves

Young rhinos are calves. A calf weighs 30 to 175 pounds (14 to 79 kilograms) at birth. The calf stands about 2 feet (61 centimeters) tall at the shoulders. A calf stays with its mother for 2 to 3 years. The mother chases her calf away after she gives birth to another calf.

Sumatran rhino

Rhinos and People

Rhinos do not have any predators. But people hunt and kill rhinos. They cut off rhinos' horns. People make medicine and tools from rhinos' horns. People clear rhinos' habitats for farming. Rhinos cannot protect themselves from people.

white rhinos

Protecting Rhinos

People around the world work to protect rhinos. Rhinos are endangered. Very few rhinos live in the wild. People build parks where rhinos are safe from hunters. They also pass laws to protect rhinos from hunters.

endangered
at risk of dying out

Hands On: The Size of a White Rhino

An adult white rhino can be as tall as 6 feet (1.8 meters). It can be about 12 feet (3.7 meters) long. You can see how large rhinos are with this activity.

What You Need

Classroom
Ruler or tape measure
Masking tape

What You Do

1. Measure 6 feet (1.8 meters) from the floor on a wall or chalkboard. You may need an adult to help you reach this height.
2. Put a piece of masking tape on the wall at this height. This is about how tall a white rhino is at the shoulder.
3. Measure 12 feet (3.7 meters) along the wall from the first mark. Put a piece of masking tape at this spot. This is about how long a white rhino is from its head to its tail.

How many white rhinos could fit around the edge of the classroom?

Words to Know

endangered (en-DAYN-jurd)—at risk of dying out; rhinos are endangered.

habitat (HAB-uh-tat)—the place where an animal lives

herbivore (HUR-buh-vor)—an animal that eats only plants

keratin (KAIR-uh-tin)—the substance that makes up hair and fingernails; a rhino's horn is made of keratin.

mammal (MAM-uhl)—a warm-blooded animal that has a backbone and feeds milk to its young

predator (PRED-uh-tur)—an animal that hunts and eats other animals

warm-blooded (warm-BLUHD-id)—having a body temperature that stays the same

Read More

Holmes, Kevin J. *Rhinos.* Animals. Mankato, Minn.: Bridgestone Books, 2000.

Murray, Peter. *Rhinos.* Chanhassen, Minn.: Child's World, 2001.

Stewart, Melissa. *Rhinoceroses.* New York: Children's Press, 2002.

Internet Sites

International Rhino Foundation
http://www.rhinos-irf.org/rhinos
San Antonio Zoo—Rhinoceros
http://www.sazoo-aq.org/rhino.html
SOS Rhino—Rhinos Facts and Resources
http://www.sosrhino.org/facts/index.html

Index